Seed to Plant

Melvin and Gilda Berger

SCHOLASTIC INC.
New York Toronto London Auckland Sydney
Mexico City New Delhi Hong Kong Buenos Aires

Photographs: Cover: Dwight Kuhn; p. 1: John Kaprielian/Photo Researchers, Inc.;
p. 3: David Young-Wolff/PhotoEdit;
p. 4: Jerome Wexler/Photo Researchers, Inc.; (inset) Stephen Kline/Bruce Coleman, Inc.;
p. 5: Jay Freis/The Image Bank/Getty Images; p. 6: Dwight Kuhn; p. 7: Dwight Kuhn;
p. 8: Dwight Kuhn; p. 9: Dwight Kuhn; p. 10: Stephen J. Krasemann/Photo Researchers, Inc.;
p. 11: Stephen J. Krasemann/Photo Researchers, Inc.;
p. 12: John Kaprielian/Photo Researchers, Inc.; p. 13: E.R. Degginger/Photo Researchers, Inc.;
p. 14: Dwight Kuhn; p. 15: Cassy Cohen/PhotoEdit; p. 16: Michael Newman/PhotoEdit

Photo Research: Sarah Longacre

ISBN 0-439-57486-2

12 11 10 9 8 7 6 5 4 3   4 5 6 7 8 9/0
                                                               08

Printed in the U.S.A.
First printing, March 2004

A seed can grow into a plant.

Some seeds are tiny.

Some seeds are very big.

You put a seed in the ground.

Fun Fact

Most seeds contain food to help the new plant grow.

A little plant starts to grow.

Fun Fact
The new plant starts to grow roots and leaves.

The plant grows down.

The plant grows up.

The plant grows and grows.

Fun Fact
To grow, most plants
need soil, water, air,
and sunshine.

It grows down and it grows up.

The plant may make a flower.

The flower makes seeds.

Fun Fact

The pits in plums, cherries, and peaches are seeds.

The flower may make a fruit.

Many fruits have seeds inside.

Each seed can grow into a plant.